Devotions to Leave You Smiling

Devotions to Leave You
Smiling

Brian Kelley Bauknight
Illustrated by John McPherson

DIMENSIONS
FOR LIVING
NASHVILLE

DEVOTIONS TO LEAVE YOU SMILING

This book is printed on acid-free paper.

Library of Congress Cataloging-in-Publication Data
Bauknight, Brian Kelley, 1939-
    Devotions to leave you smiling / Brian Kelley Bauknight; illustrated by John McPherson.
       p. cm.
    ISBN 0-687-05290-4 (pbk. : alk. paper)
       1. Devotional literature, English.   2. Christian life—Humor.   I. Title.
    BV4832.3 .B38 2002
    242—dc21

2001007673

02 03 04 05 06 07 08 09 10 11—10 9 8 7 6 5 4 3 2 1

MANUFACTURED IN THE UNITED STATES OF AMERICA

To the members and friends

of Christ United Methodist Church,

Bethel Park, Pennsylvania,who have both endured

and encouraged these stories in the laughter of hope

for more than twenty years

"Smiling faces make you happy, and good news makes you feel better." (Proverbs 15:30 TEV)

*   *   *   *   *   *

"Then Abraham fell on his face and laughed . . ."
(Genesis 17:17)

Contents

Introduction

God intends for us to smile. Far more muscles are used when we frown than when we smile. So why overwork facial muscles? Laughter is as much a part of the heart of God as are tears.

One of my favorite paintings shows Jesus playing with children. Jesus' head is thrown back in the uproarious laughter of delight at the antics or comments of the children. Gospel writers record that Jesus participated in a joyous wedding feast. I hear laughter echoing through the centuries from other tables around which Jesus sat as an invited guest. Serious conversation took place, to be sure. But laughter must have occurred as well. When Jesus ate lunch at the home of Zacchaeus in Jericho; when he shared meals with Mary, Martha, and Lazarus; when he visited at the home of Peter; even when he ate with "tax collectors and sinners," the room must surely have been filled with joy and laughter—sometimes, so much so that Jesus was mocked by his enemies (see Luke 7:34)!

Humorous stories permeate my preaching and teaching ministry—especially in the past ten years. The stories presented here are collected or adapted from friends and colleagues, from conversations, from a variety of newsletters, and from oral tradition. Humor is the common property of all. Humorous stories that illustrate or illuminate the gospel are passed from person to person for moments of lighthearted sharing. Often the end result can be profound and insightful.

This book is a collection of devotions built around some of the lighter fare of life. Each devotion presented here begins with a *smile*. Each includes a Scripture reference. And each concludes with a "sendoff"— a prayer, challenge, or thought for the day. I encourage you not to read too many of the devotions at one time; give yourself time to enjoy each story, each Scripture, and each sendoff.

I invite you into the lighter side of spirituality as you use this book. Let God's gift of smiles and laughter light up your life. Join me in the laughter of incredible hope. May such smiles of hope bring you closer to the One who is the Light of the world.

Brian Kelley Bauknight

1. Simple Directions

*L*ost on a back road in Alabama, a motorist asked the way to Montgomery. An old farmer sitting on the fence looked down the road, scratched his head, and gave explicit instructions. Half an hour later, after carefully following the farmer's directions, the motorist found himself back at the starting point. The farmer was still sitting on the fence in placid contemplation of the landscape.

"Hey, what's the idea?" the motorist demanded. "I did just what you told me, and look where I wound up!"

"Well, young feller," the farmer explained, "I didn't aim to waste my time telling you how to get to Montgomery until I found out if you could follow simple directions!"

Scripture: The law of the LORD is perfect, reviving the soul; / the decrees of the LORD are sure, making wise the simple. (Psalm 19:7)

Sendoff: Prayerfully claim a clear sense of direction for your life, always looking toward Jesus for insight and instruction.

2. Ice Fishing

A man who loved to go ice fishing went out onto a big slab of ice and started cutting a hole in it. Suddenly, he heard a voice speaking above him, saying, "Young man, save your time and energy. There are no fish down there." So the man pulled up his saw and went to another place several yards away. As he was sawing a hole in the ice, that same voice boomed from above and said, "Don't waste your time and energy there either! You won't find any fish down there at all."

The determined fisherman pulled up his saw and went to a third location. A third time, the voice spoke and said, "I'm telling you, sir, you are wasting your time!"

The young man looked up and said, "Okay, okay, I hear you! Who *are* you, anyway? God?"

And the voice from above said, "No, I'm the manager of the ice-skating rink."

> Scripture: *When he had finished speaking, he said to Simon, "Put out into the deep water and let down your nets for a catch." Simon answered, "Master, we have worked all night long but have caught nothing. Yet if you say so, I will let down the nets." When they had done this, they caught so many fish that their nets were beginning to break. (Luke 5:4-6)*
>
> Sendoff: *Help me, Master, to do my fishing in the right places.*

3. Give Thanks

*T*wo Boy Scouts were on a hike in the woods. One of them came upon some fresh bear tracks. The two decided to follow the tracks and perhaps catch a glimpse of a live bear in the wild. The path took them into a small ravine. Once in the ravine, they discovered that the opposite end was blocked.

As they turned around to retrace their steps, they found themselves face-to-face with a huge, hungry black bear. Terrified, they fell to their knees in prayer. "Lord," they prayed, "please save us from this bear."

When they opened their eyes, they saw the bear on his haunches, in prayer as well. "He's a *Christian* bear!" cried one Scout. "We're *saved!*"

"I don't think so," said the other. "Listen!"

And the bear prayed: "Lord, for that which I am about to receive from thy bounty, I give you thanks."

> *Scripture: All your works shall give thanks to you, O Lord, / and all your faithful shall bless you. (Psalm 145:10)*
>
> *Sendoff: Give thanks to God for some specific "bounty" in your life.*

4. Love God

a child's view of the Old Testament message: "Love God 365 days a year—and be careful not to take too many days off."

> *Scripture: Love the LORD your God with all your heart and with all your soul and with all your strength. (Deuteronomy 6:5 NIV)*
>
> *Sendoff: God, help me love you throughout this day. Help me know how to express that love from deep within. Teach me to extend that love to others.*

5. Stay Alert

A small boy was told he was too young to wear a watch. But he continued to plead for one, until the whole family grew weary of his begging. Finally, his father, after explaining that he could have a watch when he was older, forbade him to mention the subject again.

The next Sunday, the children in the family—as was their custom—repeated Bible verses at the Sunday breakfast table. When it was the boy's turn, he astonished them all with a rendering of Mark 13:37: "What I say unto you, I say unto all: watch!"

Scripture: Keep alert, stand firm in your faith, be courageous, be strong. (1 Corinthians 16:13)

Sendoff: Ask God to keep you alert for opportunities to speak a word of hope to someone today.

6. Know Where You Are!

*T*wo New Yorkers were driving through Louisiana. As they were approaching the town of Natchitoches, they started arguing about the pronunciation of the name.

Upon stopping at a fast-food establishment for lunch, the New Yorker who was driving asked the manager, "Before we order, could you please settle an argument for us? Would you please pronounce where we are—very slowly and very clearly?"

The manager leaned over the counter, smiled, and said, "Burrrrrr-gerrrrr-Kiiiing."

Scripture: Thomas said to him, "Lord, we don't know where you are going, so how can we know the way?" Jesus answered, "I am the way and the truth and the life. No one comes to the Father except through me." (John 14:5-6 NIV)

Sendoff: Lord, let me be clear about who I am and where I am with you. Let that clarity shine forth from me in every way.

7. Blessed Are the Meek

a man was sitting in the waiting room of a doctor's office. From the other side of the door he heard a voice, shouting, "Typhoid! Tetanus! Measles! Flu!" Finally, he asked the nurse at the desk what was going on.

The nurse replied, "Oh, that's just the doctor. Around here, he likes to call all the shots."

Scripture: "Blessed are the meek, / for they will inherit the earth." (Matthew 5:5 NIV)

Sendoff: God, give me grace to be humble, and to know the limitations of my own humanity. May others know that I am your child.

8. Let It Rain

A couple who had been married for ten years wanted to take a very special second honeymoon. They decided to go to the Smoky Mountains. They made arrangements for someone to care for their two small children and set out for a rustic lodge in the mountains. They loved to hike and walk the trails, and they looked forward to the week with great anticipation.

On the first morning there, they appeared on the porch of the lodge in their hiking gear only to discover that it had begun to rain. Disappointed but hopeful, they sat down on the porch, reasonably sure that the rain would end in an hour or so. But the rain continued—two hours, four, then eight. Obviously, they were not going to be able to hike that day.

Somewhat frustrated at the ruined day, they retired for the night in hopes of the next day being better. It rained again. And the third day. And the fourth day. All week it rained.

Finally, their vacation came to an end and they stood with their bags packed on the porch, ready to return home. They were angry and upset at being unable to enjoy this long-awaited vacation.

As they stood on the porch, they saw an old mountaineer sitting on a rocking chair not far away. They remembered that they had seen him almost every day in that chair. His feet were propped up on the banister, and he was just sitting there watching it rain.

The couple struck up a conversation with him. At one point, the young man asked: "How can you be so calm and collected? Doesn't all this rain get to you?"

The older man's reply was simple and profound: "Oh, no," he said, "the rain doesn't bother me at all. You see, years ago I decided that when it starts to rain, I'd just let it."

Scripture: May you be made strong with all the strength that comes from his glorious power, and may you be prepared to endure everything with patience, while joyfully giving thanks to the Father, who has enabled you to share in the inheritance of the saints in the light. (Colossians 1:11-12)

Sendoff: Lord, whatever this day brings, may I patiently give you thanks for being in my life.

9. The Banquet

a woman was the emcee of a banquet and was getting quite anxious when the pastor was late and it was time to offer the invocation. Frantically, she began looking around the crowd to see if there was another minister present. There was none. Desperately, she turned to her husband and asked him to fill in. He was visibly shaken.

But he stood up and announced, reverently, "Since there are no clergy present, let us give thanks . . . "

Scripture: Since we are receiving a kingdom that cannot be shaken, let us give thanks. (Hebrews 12:28)

Sendoff: Giving thanks is always and everywhere appropriate for all. Pray a prayer of thanks right now.

10. An Encouraging Word

*T*wo cowboys were out on the range herding a group of buffalo. One cowboy turned to the other and said, "These buffalo are the dirtiest, smelliest, ugliest creatures on the face of the earth."

Whereupon one buffalo turned to another and said, "I thought out here we weren't supposed to hear a discouraging word."

Scripture: Therefore encourage one another and build up each other, as indeed you are doing. (1 Thessalonians 5:11)

Sendoff: Watch for someone today who needs or deserves an encouraging word from you. Readily offer that word, and give thanks for the opportunity.

11. Age of Wisdom

*O*n his son's twenty-first birthday, a father gave him a beautiful gold pocket watch. His presentation speech, in full, was as follows: "Son, we had always planned to give you this watch when you reached the age of wisdom; we've decided it's better not to wait."

Scripture: ... until all of us come to the unity of the faith and of the knowledge of the Son of God, to maturity, to the measure of the full stature of Christ. (Ephesians 4:13)

Sendoff: God, give me a growing maturity in the faith, sufficient for my own journey.

12. Promises Kept

a college student walked into a photographer's studio with a framed picture of his girlfriend. He asked if the picture could be duplicated. The photographer removed the photo from the frame and noticed the inscription written on the reverse side. It read, "My dearest Tom: I love you with all my heart. I love you more and more each day. I will love you forever. I am yours for all eternity." It was signed, "Diane."

Then, there was a P.S.: "If we ever break up, I want this picture back."

Scripture: For in him every one of God's promises is a "Yes." For this reason it is through him that we say the "Amen," to the glory of God. (2 Corinthians 1:20)

Sendoff: O God, may I know the treasure of your promises to me—promises that endure in Jesus.

13. From the Mouths of Children

The day was blistering hot and muggy. The house was full of guests, and things were not going well. Finally, the hostess got everyone seated for dinner and asked her seven-year-old daughter to offer the blessing. "But, Mother," said the child, "I don't know what to say."

"Yes, you do," said her mother. "Just say the last prayer you heard me use."

Obediently, the child bowed her head and recited hesitantly: "O Lord, why did I invite all these people to dinner on such a hot day?"

Scripture: Jesus was praying in a certain place. When he finished, one of his disciples said to him, "Lord, teach us to pray." (Luke 11:1 NIV)

Sendoff: Lord, help me to learn to pray with the honesty and assurance of a child.

14. Wedding Cake

a cake maker took an order for a wedding cake from a couple about to be married. The couple requested a verse inscribed on the cake, taken from 1 John 4:18: "There is no fear in love, but perfect love casts out fear."

The baker must have misread the order. When the cake arrived on the day of the wedding, the newlyweds were aghast to find that the "1" had been dropped from the Scripture reference. Instead, the verse that appeared was from John 4:18, which reads: "For you have had five husbands, and the one you now have is not your husband."

Scripture: Let marriage be held in honor by all. (Hebrews 13:4)

Sendoff: Think of a married couple whom you know well. Offer a prayer on their behalf right now.

15. Some Things Cannot Be Risked

*T*wo individuals were driving down a highway in a large truck. They came to a bridge underpass with a big, stern sign in front of it reading "Absolutely no vehicles over 10 feet 3 inches allowed." The two men pulled over to the shoulder and got out of the truck with a measuring tape. As it turned out, the truck was 10 feet 4 inches tall. At this point, the second man looked at the driver and said, "What shall we do?"

The driver glanced both ways and then answered, "There's not a policeman in sight. Let's risk it!"

Scripture: For we intend to do what is right not only in the Lord's sight but also in the sight of others. (2 Corinthians 8:21)

Sendoff: Lord, help me to make all decisions this day as one who lives ever in your sight.

16. Briefly Noted

$\mathcal{A}$ bishop called a gathering of all the ministers in his area for a one-day consultation and retreat. The man assigned for the opening devotions that day called in sick at the last minute. The bishop sought out a young man who had recently graduated from the seminary and had just been ordained. The bishop explained what had happened, and then he asked this young clergyman to lead the morning devotions.

"Oh, Bishop," he exclaimed, "I could not do that. I have nothing prepared. I would not know what to say."

The bishop handed the young man his own Bible. "Here, take my Bible and spend a few minutes of quiet time somewhere doing your preparation. Then, just trust the Lord. Just trust the Lord."

The young man knew he could not refuse the bishop a second time. He reluctantly took the Bible and began to leaf through the pages. He could not find a proper text, but he did find a number of papers in the Bible with notes on them. One piece of paper intrigued him. As he looked it over, he decided that it would provide a good outline for a morning devotional for the group.

The young clergyman presented the devotions with exceptional poise and grace. When he was finished, the bishop came running over to him. Expecting some kind of gracious response, instead he heard the bishop exclaim, "Young man! What do you think you are doing? You used my notes for the closing worship today. Now what shall I do for my own leadership later on?"

The younger man looked at his bishop and counseled, "Just trust the Lord, Bishop. Just trust the Lord."

Scripture: "When they hand you over, do not worry about how you are to speak or what you are to say; for what you are to say will be given to you at that time; for it is not you who speak, but the Spirit of your Father speaking through you." (Matthew 10:19-20)

Sendoff: God, grant me the appropriate inspirited words each time I speak to someone today.

17. Fear

A little girl caught her father off guard one day with one of those outrageous question-asking sessions in which children engage. "Daddy," she said, "Are you afraid of wild animals?"

The father replied with paternal boast, "No, of course not."

"Well, Daddy, are you afraid of the dark?"

"Never," said the father bravely.

"Daddy, are you afraid of the long woolly worms?"

"Never!" said the father, feeling more invincible with each reply he made.

"Well, Daddy," the little girl concluded after a brief pause, "then you aren't afraid of anything but Mommy, right?"

Scripture: The fear of the LORD is the beginning of wisdom, / and knowledge of the Holy One is understanding. (Proverbs 9:10 NIV)

Sendoff: Lord, teach me to stand in fear and awe of you and you alone.

18. The Speed of Time

a rather harried preacher, speaking to his congregation on a Sunday morning, said, "The philosophy of ministry that worked in the sixties didn't work in the seventies. What worked in the seventies didn't work in the eighties. And what worked in the eighties didn't work in the nineties. We are now in a new decade and a new millennium. Let's hope that what worked in our first service will still work in the second!"

Scripture: I will bless the LORD at all times; / his praise shall continually be in my mouth. (Psalm 34:1)

Sendoff: In the midst of sudden or gradual change, help me, O God, to be ready to praise you at all times.

19. The Need for Light

a small, poor congregation of believers in Appalachia scrimped and saved enough money together to begin building a church for themselves. When they had finished the basement, they had to cap it off and suspend building because they had run out of funds. The basement was quite dark, as the small windows allowed very little in the way of natural light.

The young pastor called a meeting and suggested that the church should buy a chandelier. Immediately, a crusty, older member from the back of the room stood and objected. "I have three good reasons *not* to buy a chandelier," he said. "First, no one here knows how to *spell* it. So how can we order one? Second, if we *did* get one, no one could *play* it. And third, but most important, what we *really* need around here is more *light.*"

Scripture: When Jesus spoke again to the people, he said, "I am the light of the world. Whoever follows me will never walk in darkness, but will have the light of life." (John 8:12 NIV)

Sendoff: Lord, help me to see in you an all-sufficient Light.

20. Get a Grip

I thought I had a handle on life, but then the handle fell off.

> *Scripture: Let love be genuine; hate what is evil, hold fast to what is good. (Romans 12:9)*
>
> *Sendoff: Gracious God, help me hold fast to the good this day.*

21. Nice Day

$\mathcal{A}$ man went into the drugstore. From the shelves he selected a bottle of extra-strength ibuprofen, twelve ounces of laxative, an elastic knee support, a supply of corn plasters, some sinus medication, a vaporizer, a remedy for sore gums, and a tube of hemorrhoidal cream. He took these items to the counter, where they were totaled on the register. He could scarcely believe his ears when the clerk handed him the sackful of items and said, "Have a nice day!"

Scripture: Strengthen the weak hands, / and make firm the feeble knees. (Isaiah 35:3)

Sendoff: God, give me physical strength, mobility, and freedom from pain sufficient for this day.

22. Office Motto

*M*any offices have little plaques on the wall that express certain mottoes for the office staff. Two different offices recently displayed the same plaque, perhaps expressing the sentiments of many on the work force there. The plaque read: One day I shall burst my buds of calm and blossom fully into hysteria.

Scripture: For thus said the LORD GOD, *the Holy One of Israel: / In returning and rest you shall be saved; / in quietness and in trust shall be your strength. (Isaiah 30:15)*

Sendoff: Help me, Lord, to find an active serenity in simply knowing you.

23. First and Last

a mother was preparing pancakes for her sons, Kevin, five, and Ryan, three. The boys began to argue over who would get the first pancake. Their mother saw the opportunity for a moral lesson. "If Jesus were sitting here, he would say, 'Let my brother have the first pancake. I can wait.'"

Kevin turned to his younger brother and said, "Ryan, you be Jesus."

Scripture: But many who are first will be last, and the last will be first. (Mark 10:31)

Sendoff: Find a way to prefer the lowest place today rather than the highest.

24. Better-looking

*G*randpa and granddaughter were sitting in her room when she asked, "Grandpa, did God make you?"

"Yes, child, God made me," he answered.

"And Grandpa, did God make me?" Again the answer was yes.

The little girl looked into the mirror for a while, then said, "You know, Grandpa, God is doing a whole lot better work lately!"

Scripture: For it was you who formed my inward parts; / you knit me together in my mother's womb. / I praise you, for I am fearfully and wonderfully made. / Wonderful are your works; / that I know very well. (Psalm 139:13-14)

Sendoff: God's creation of humankind is truly remarkable and wondrous. You are a special part of that divine effort.

25. Secret Service

a man was leaving church one Sunday. He stopped in front of the preacher to shake hands. The preacher grabbed the man's hand and pulled him aside. The pastor enjoined, "You need to join the army of the Lord!"

The man replied, "I'm *already* in the army of the Lord, Pastor."

The minister then questioned, "Then why do I not see you here more often? Why not more than Christmas and Easter?"

The man whispered back, "I'm in the Secret Service."

Scripture: Enter his gates with thanksgiving, / and his courts with praise; / give thanks to him and praise his name. (Psalm 100:4 NIV)

Sendoff: Worship is the believer's vital breath. Worship is the energizing center for a life of discipleship.

26. Corps of Engineers

*A*fter church one day, a mother asked her young son, "What was your Sunday school lesson about today?"

"We learned about Moses leading the people of Israel across the Red Sea," came the reply.

"Tell me the story," the mother requested.

After a few thoughtful seconds, the boy said, "Well, Moses called out his corps of engineers, and they inflated a whole platoon of life rafts. Then they lashed them together to make a bridge across the sea. The Israelites walked across. When they saw the Egyptians following them, Moses directed his bow and arrow sharpshooters to fire at the rafts. The rafts sank in the sea, and all the Egyptians drowned."

"Now, Billy," said his mother. "You know that's not the way the story happened."

"I know, Mom, but if I repeated it the way my Sunday school teacher told it, you'd never believe it!"

Scripture: Then Moses stretched out his hand over the sea, and all that night the Lord drove the sea back with a strong east wind and turned it into dry land. The waters were divided, and the Israelites went through the sea on dry ground, with a wall of water on their right and on their left. (Exodus 14:21-22 NIV)

Sendoff: Walk today with the God of amazing miracles!

27. Give Me Some Skin!

a young boy was in his bed for the night when a storm broke and awakened him. He called out to his father in fear. The father came to the room to calm his son's fears. "It's all right, Son," he said. "God is with you."

"I know that, Daddy," said the boy, "but I need somebody with *skin!*"

> *Scripture: The Word became flesh and lived among us, and we have seen his glory, the glory as of a father's only son, full of grace and truth. (John 1:14)*
>
> *Sendoff: God knows I need the Holy Presence in the midst of this life. May I sense that Presence somewhere today.*

28. Measuring Up

$\mathcal{A}$ group of chickens lived in a barnyard. Some boys were playing football nearby, and the football accidentally landed in the middle of the chicken yard. The old rooster took a long look at this object that had made an intrusion into their area, and he then called the chickens together. He said, "I want you to take note of what some of the chickens in other places are doing!"

Scripture: For where there is envy and selfish ambition, there will also be disorder and wickedness of every kind. (James 3:16)

Sendoff: God, grant me deep peace and contentment without envy or jealousy of any other person or lifestyle.

29. Broken Pottery

a woman had kept a very fine antique vase in her home that was passed down from generation to generation. It sat in a place of honor beside the fireplace. One day her nine-year-old daughter came to her. "Mommy, you know that vase that has been passed down from generation to generation?" Her mother acknowledged that she did know the vase. "Well, Mommy, *this* generation just broke it."

Scripture: But we have this treasure in clay jars, so that it may be made clear that this extraordinary power belongs to God and does not come from us. (2 Corinthians 4:7)

Sendoff: God, let me trust not in valuable "things" or "stuff," but only in your power and grace in my life.

30. Answering Machine

A college student had a telephone answering machine in his dorm room. "Hi, this is Dave," went the outgoing message. "If it's Mom or Dad, please send money. If it's a friend, you still owe me money. If it's the student-loan office, you didn't loan me enough money. If it's a female, leave your number and I'll call you back soon; and don't worry, I have plenty of money."

> *Scripture: You shall eat in plenty and be satisfied, / and praise the name of the LORD your God, who has dealt wondrously with you. (Joel 2:26)*
>
> *Sendoff: You are a God of plenty. By your grace, I shall always have enough.*

31. Vice Presidential Material?

*T*he new vice president was flaunting his title so much, one of his coworkers finally said to him, "These days, vice presidents are a dime a dozen. In fact, the title is getting so ridiculous that my supermarket even has a vice president in charge of peas." The new vice president was insulted and skeptical. So he phoned the supermarket and asked for the vice president of peas. The voice at the other end of the line asked, *"Canned* or *frozen?"*

> *Scripture: "All who exalt themselves will be humbled, and all who humble themselves will be exalted." (Matthew 23:12)*
>
> *Sendoff: Lord, let me be humble in my service to you.*

32. The Innkeeper

A seven-year-old boy was in the Christmas play in his church. He was given the part of the innkeeper. When Joseph and Mary came to the door, Joseph would knock on the door, and this little boy was to open the door and say, "There's no room in the inn," and then close the door.

He went home and told his parents about the play, but he said he didn't like his part at all. He didn't like telling Mary and Joseph there was no room in the inn. His parents tried to encourage him by explaining that this was a very important part of the story. It was in the Bible. They read it to him. Still, he didn't like the part.

The night before the play, his parents went to the rehearsal. The boy took his place at the right time. Joseph and Mary came up, and Joseph knocked on the door. The boy opened the door and said, "There is no room in the inn," and closed the door. Then he opened the door again and said, "But would you like to come in for a snack?"

Scripture: The word is very near to you; it is in your mouth and in your heart for you to observe. (Deuteronomy 30:14)

Sendoff: Come into my heart, Lord Jesus. There is room in my heart for you.

33. The Broom

A woman was traveling on a steep, winding mountain road. In the course of her travel, she drew close behind a small-paneled truck that was struggling up the steep grade. Finally the truck could go no farther and came to a complete stop. The driver jumped out of the truck with a broom in his hand and began beating against the side of the truck for a few seconds. Then he hopped back into the cab and drove on up the hill.

A few minutes later the truck slowed again. Again it ground to a stop. And again the man jumped out, broom in hand, and beat on the side panel once more. Then he returned to the front and drove on.

A third time, the same thing happened. Finally the woman could stand it no longer. When the driver jumped out of his seat, she got out of her car as well. "Sir, I simply have to ask," she said. "Why on earth do you stop your vehicle, get out, and beat on the side with a broom every so often?"

"Well, I'll tell you," replied the man. "This is a half-ton truck. And I am carrying one ton of canaries. The only way I have any chance of getting them to their destination is by keeping at least half of them in the air most of the time!"

Scripture: "Come to me, all you that are weary and are carrying heavy burdens, and I will give you rest." (Matthew 11:28)

Sendoff: Only you, O God, can make the rough going smooth. I celebrate your readiness to do that for me.

34. Mystery Is Mystery!

a bishop tells of the time when his children were very young and he was serving a local church in the early years of his ministry. One Christmas Eve, he and his family headed to church for the candlelight service. His son looked over at him and said, "Dad, are you going to let us enjoy the Christmas story this year, or are you going to try to *explain* it to everyone?"

Scripture: Think of us in this way, as servants of Christ and stewards of God's mysteries. (1 Corinthians 4:1)

Sendoff: What joy comes in celebrating the mysteries of Christmas!

35. Urgent Call

*H*urry!" the doctor cried out to his teenage daughter. "Put my stethoscope and my medicine bag into my car. I just received an emergency call from someone who said she will die if I don't come immediately!"

"Oh, Daddy, that call wasn't for you," the daughter replied. "That call was for me!"

Scripture: And let people learn to devote themselves to good works in order to meet urgent needs, so that they may not be unproductive. (Titus 3:14)

Sendoff: Always be ready to respond to an urgent prompting from God. Have you received one lately? Are you open to God's prompting?

36. Whispering

Two children were playing together in their room. Their mother stopped in for a moment. "What are you playing?" she asked?

"We're playing 'church,'" came the reply.

"'Church'? Then why are you whispering? You're not supposed to whisper in church!"

"It's okay, Mom—we're in the choir."

Scripture: For in the days of David and Asaph long ago there was a leader of the singers, and there were songs of praise and thanksgiving to God. (Nehemiah 12:46)

Sendoff: Give thanks to God for those who have the spiritual gift of singing as an offering in the church.

37. Outdoor Life

a seventy-five-year-old man went to his doctor for a physical. The doctor was amazed at not finding a thing wrong with him. The doctor said, "You really have the body of a man twenty-five years younger. What's your secret?"

The man explained: "Well, when my wife and I were married fifty years ago, we made an agreement. We decided that we would never quarrel. So when we have a difference of opinion that is potentially explosive, and we see a fight coming on, she just stays in the house and I go out for a long walk. I guess my good health is due to the fact that for fifty years, I've pretty much lived an outdoor life."

Scripture: Be angry but do not sin; do not let the sun go down on your anger, and do not make room for the devil. (Ephesians 4:26-27)

Sendoff: Do you have any creative, God-inspired ways to deal with anger or serious disagreements?

38. Binding Questions

a young bridegroom, standing in front of the altar with his bride, listened intently to the decisive question asked in King James Bible elegance: "Wilt thou have this woman to be thy wife?"

With adoring eyes fixed upon her radiant splendor, he replied proudly, "I wilt."

Scripture: Above all, my beloved, do not swear, either by heaven or by earth or by any other oath, but let your "Yes" be yes and your "No" be no. (James 5:12)

Sendoff: If you are married, call your spouse right now and tell him or her how glad you are that you married him or her; if not right now, do so before this day is over!

39. Beyond a Tithe

a pastor was concluding one of his best ever sermons on tithing. The conviction level was high throughout the congregation. One of the deacons was so overwhelmed by the pastor's exhortation, he was inspired to help. The deacon leapt to his feet and said, "One tenth is not enough; each of us should give a *twentieth!*"

Scripture: Bring the full tithe into the storehouse, so that there may be food in my house, and thus put me to the test, says the LORD of hosts; see if I will not open the windows of heaven for you and pour down for you an overflowing blessing. (Malachi 3:10)

Sendoff: To tithe is to be stretched toward true discipleship. Tithing means learning to trust God.

40. The Unpacking

a little girl was helping her mother unpack the family's Nativity scene and set it up. As she unpacked each of the pieces, she said, "Here are Mary and Joseph; here are the shepherds; here are the animals." When she got to the figurine of Jesus in the manger, she said, "And here is the Baby Jesus in his car seat."

Scripture: And she gave birth to her firstborn son and wrapped him in bands of cloth, and laid him in a manger. (Luke 2:7)

Sendoff: Don't miss the lighter side of a child's observations.

41. A Couple of Nuts

On the outskirts of town, there was a large old pecan tree by the cemetery fence. One day, two boys filled up a bucketful of nuts and sat down by the tree, out of sight, and began dividing the nuts. "One for you, one for me. One for you, one for me," said one boy.

In the process, several of the nuts were dropped and rolled down toward the fence. Another boy came riding along the road on his bicycle. As he passed, he thought he heard voices from inside the cemetery, and he slowed down to investigate. Sure enough, he heard "One for you, one for me. One for you, one for me." He just knew what it was. "Oh, my!" he shuddered, "It's Satan and the Lord dividing souls at the cemetery!"

The boy jumped back on his bike and rode off. Just around the bend, he met an old man with a cane, hobbling along. "Come here, quick!" said the boy. "You won't believe what I heard! Satan and the Lord are down at the cemetery dividing up the souls!" The man said, "Beat it, kid, can't you see it's hard for me to walk?" When the boy insisted, though, the man hobbled to the cemetery.

Standing by the fence, they heard, "One for you, one for me. One for you, one for me." The old man whispered, "Boy, you've been tellin' the truth! Let's see if we can see the devil himself." Shaking with fear, they peered through the fence, yet they were still unable to see anything. The old man and the boy gripped the wrought-iron bars of the fence tighter and tighter as they tried to get a glimpse of Satan.

At last, they heard, "One for you, one for me. And one last one for you. That's all. Now, let's go get those nuts by the fence, and we'll be done!"

Scripture: But who can endure the day of his coming, and who can stand when he appears? For he is like a refiner's fire and like fullers' soap. (Malachi 3:2)

Sendoff: Lord, help me withstand the powers of evil and live a holy, grace-filled life.

42. Long-winded

a guest preacher was delivering his message at a special gathering. He got a bit carried away and talked for two hours. Finally he realized what he was doing and said, "I'm sorry I talked so long. I left my watch at home."

Came a reply from the back of the room, "There is a *calendar* behind you!"

Scripture: Conduct yourselves wisely toward outsiders, making the most of the time. (Colossians 4:5)

Sendoff: Let all of my time and all that I say honor you, O God.

43. Wise Words

*W*hen you are in over your head, there is no better time to keep your mouth shut.

Scripture: Remind them to be subject to rulers and authorities, to be obedient, to be ready for every good work, to speak evil of no one, to avoid quarreling, to be gentle, and to show every courtesy to everyone. (Titus 3:1-2)

Sendoff: Lord, let the words that I speak bear the wisdom of your Spirit and the power of your love.

44. Old and Rich

*D*uring the hectic Christmas rush, a harried woman was seeking a parking place in a crowded shopping center. One finally opened up. However, as she was maneuvering her large black car into the space, a young man in a small sports car sneaked in ahead of her. As he jumped out of his car, the woman got out of her car and shouted to him, "Why did you do that?"

"Because I am young and fast!" came the reply. Then he disappeared into a nearby camera shop.

This very dignified-looking lady, obviously fuming and sputtering to herself, got back into her large black sedan and proceeded to ram the small sports car with her large vehicle, again and again. A crowd gathered as she knocked his car around. The young man came running out of the camera store yelling at her. "Hey! What's going on? What do you think you are *doing*?"

Calmly, the woman stepped out of her car and faced him down. "You may be young and fast, but I am *old* and *rich*."

Scripture: The wealth of the rich is their strong city; / in their imagination it is like a high wall. (Proverbs 18:11)

Sendoff: May I never use affluence to impress or one-up another.

45. Short Sermon

The pastor preached a very short sermon one Sunday morning. He explained: "My dog got into my office and chewed up some of my notes."

At the close of the service, a visitor made his request: "If your dog ever has puppies, please let my pastor have one of them."

Scripture: See, the LORD's hand is not too short to save, / nor his ear too dull to hear. (Isaiah 59:1)

Sendoff: Lord, let me be brief and concise when such is your best way.

46. An Embarrassing Moment

A car was involved in an accident. As expected, a large crowd gathered. A newspaper reporter, anxious to get his story, could not get near the car. Being a clever sort, he started shouting loudly, "Let me through! Let me through! I'm the son of the victim!" The crowd made way for him. Lying in front of the car was a donkey.

Scripture: [Jesus said], "All who exalt themselves will be humbled, but all who humble themselves will be exalted." (Luke 18:14)

Sendoff: Lord, give me the gracious gift of humility in all my dealings this day. Let me never feel more important than I am. Let me never display a haughty spirit.

47. Teakettle

*O*ne person's definition of *optimism:* "A cheerful frame of mind that enables a teakettle to sing even though in hot water up to its nose."

Scripture: Finally, be strong in the Lord and in his mighty power. (Ephesians 6:10 NIV)

Sendoff: Give me courage in all things, O Lord. Help me to stand tall and joyful, even in adversity.

48. Saving the Earth

a Sunday school kindergarten teacher had prepared a very fine lesson on the subject of Christian discipleship. The lesson included a game, a song, and a story. At the close of the lesson she asked for questions. Several of the children waved their hands wildly, proving to the teacher that the lesson had been a success. Calling upon a little girl whose arms had been waving more frantically that the rest, she asked, "What do you have to say about disciples?"

"Well," she began, "I just wanted you to know that I know a lot about disciples. Because at my house, we disciple everything. We have a disciple can for plastic, a disciple can for glass, a disciple can for paper. My mom says discipling will save the earth!"

Scripture: And pointing to his disciples, he said, "Here are my mother and my brothers! For whoever does the will of my Father in heaven is my brother and sister and mother." (Matthew 12:49-50)

Sendoff: Living as a disciple, I can make an impact upon my corner of the world.

49. When Do You Need an Answer?

*T*wo elderly women were discussing some of the problems encountered as they were growing older. One woman observed, "The worst thing about growing older is when you begin to lose your memory. I've known you since we were children, but right now I can't even remember your name. What is it?"

After a short pause, the second woman answered with her own question: "Do you need an answer on that right now?"

Scripture: As I was with Moses, so I will be with you; I will never leave you nor forsake you. (Joshua 1:5 NIV)

Sendoff: Thankfully, Lord, you do not fail to remember us—even in times of weakness, failure, or old age.

50. Successors

$\mathcal{A}$t morning worship, a pastor announced to the congregation that the bishop had just appointed him to another church. After the service, a woman came up to him and expressed her dismay at his leaving. The preacher responded, "Oh, I'm sure the bishop will send you someone who's a far better preacher and pastor than I am."

"No," said the woman, "that won't happen, and it *can't* happen."

"Why not?" he asked.

"Because," the woman said, "I've been here for five pastors now, and each one was worse than the last."

Scripture: "Therefore, O LORD, God of Israel, keep for your servant my father David that which you promised him, saying, 'There shall never fail you a successor before me to sit on the throne of Israel, if only your children look to their way, to walk before me as you have walked before me.'" (1 Kings 8:25)

Sendoff: Help me succeed by being faithful to Jesus at every turn. May such faithfulness be the mark and the measure of any success I have in this life.

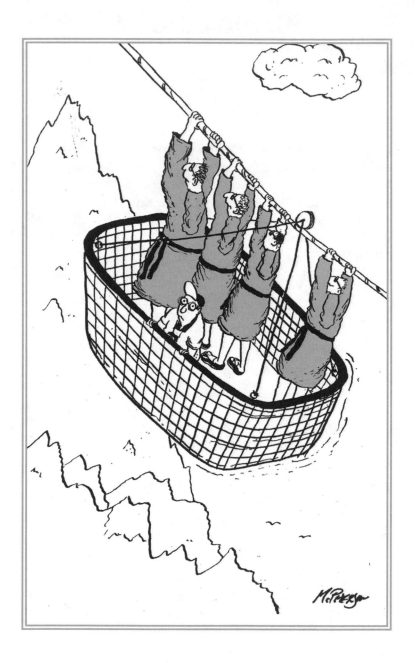

51. The Rope

a certain monastery in Portugal sits high upon a three-hundred-foot cliff. The only way the monastery can be reached is by a terrifying ride in a swaying basket that is held by a single rope, and pulled by several strong monks.

One day an American tourist was riding up in the basket and became very nervous. He noticed that the rope was quite old and frayed. He timidly asked, "How often do you change the rope?"

One monk replied, "Whenever it breaks!"

Scripture: He put a new song in my mouth, / a song of praise to our God. Many will see and fear, / and put their trust in the LORD. (Psalm 40:3)

Sendoff: God, help me to know what truly constitutes real trust in you.

52. Maturing Wisdom

A well-educated executive and his wife came to dinner parties and offered their "Ten Commandments for Parenting." Then they had their first child, followed by child number two. They then came to dinner parties with their "Eight Rules for Parenting."

Next came baby number three. They started coming to the parties with their "Five Ways to Be a Better Parent."

While they were raising three teenagers, they did not appear at the dinner parties at all. When they finally came back, shell-shocked, they had gone from their "Ten Commandments for Parenting" to "Three Suggestions That Might Work."

Scripture: Train children in the right way, / and when old, they will not stray. (Proverbs 22:6)

Sendoff: If you are a parent, pray humbly that you may be faithful in that call before God.

53. Election Options

*T*he candidate had just finished what he felt was a stirring campaign speech. "Now, are there any questions?" he asked confidently.

"Yes," said a voice from the rear. "Who else is running?"

Scripture: Peter stood up and said to them, "My brothers, you know that in the early days God made a choice among you, that I should be the one through whom the Gentiles would hear the message of the good news and become believers." (Acts 15:7)

Sendoff: Give thanks that God has chosen some to be the bearers of good news to a needy and struggling world.

54. Who Was That?

*A*fter putting her children to bed, a mother changed into old slacks and a droopy blouse and proceeded to wash her hair. As she heard the children getting more and more rambunctious, her patience grew thin. At last she threw a towel around her head and stomped into their room, putting them back into bed with stern warnings. As she left the room, she heard her three-year-old say, with a trembling voice, "Who was that?"

Scripture: Then the glory of the LORD rose up from the cherub to the threshold of the house; the house was filled with the cloud, and the court was full of the brightness of the glory of the LORD. The sound of the wings of the cherubim was heard as far as the outer court, like the voice of God Almighty when he speaks. (Ezekiel 10:4-5)

Sendoff: Sometimes it is a good thing to be startled by the authoritative voice of God.

55. Absolute Certainty

a teacher was having trouble with his bank. Neither the bank's accuracy nor its mode of expression lived up to his standards. The last straw arrived in the form of a letter from the bank, which read, "Your account appears to be overdrawn."

To this the teacher wrote back: "Please write again when you are absolutely certain."

Scripture: I know the one in whom I have put my trust, and I am sure that he is able to guard until that day what I have entrusted to him. (2 Timothy 1:12)

Sendoff: Dear God, grant to me the unfailing certainty of my faith. Give me that "blessed assurance" as a gift throughout my life.

56. Numerical Order

a student was asked to list the Ten Commandments in any order. His answer? "2, 6, 1, 8, 4, 5, 9, 3,
7, 10."

*Scripture: Know therefore that the L*ORD *your
God is God; he is the faithful God, keeping his
covenant of love to a thousand generations of
those who love him and keep his commands.
(Deuteronomy 7:9 NIV)*

*Sendoff: The Ten Commandments are God's
way of keeping order in the midst of potential
chaos. This was true in the desert in Moses'
day. It is true in our day as well.*

57. Retirement

a well-respected football coach announced his departure from coaching. He explained: "I left because of illness and fatigue: The fans were sick and tired of me."

Scripture: Jesus, tired as he was from the journey, sat down by the well. It was about the sixth hour. (John 4:6 NIV)

Sendoff: Retirement may not be included in the language of God's call. Moses began a new career at eighty. Abraham received his call at the age of seventy-five.

58. Second Shot

a golfer was addressing his ball, getting ready to hit. As he was about to swing, a voice came over the public address system: "Will the gentleman on the ladies' tee please move back to the men's tee!"

The golfer looked up for a moment, and then resumed addressing the ball. The voice came again: "Will the man on the red tees please move back to the white tees!"

The golfer looked back at the starter's shack in frustration and shouted, "Will the man on the PA be quiet so that the man on the ladies' tee can hit his second shot!"

Scripture: In the case of an athlete, no one is crowned without competing according to the rules. (2 Timothy 2:5)

Sendoff: Lord, help me always to lead with my best shot.

59. Switch

*M*iddle age is when your broad mind and narrow waist begin to change places.

Scripture: "The Son of Man has come eating and drinking, and you say, 'Look, a glutton and a drunkard, a friend of tax collectors and sinners!' Nevertheless, wisdom is vindicated by all her children." (Luke 7:34-35)

Sendoff: Wisdom means understanding the normal changes in our bodies as we grow older. Faithfulness is more substantive than body shape.

60. Optimist and Pessimist

*A*n optimist and a pessimist were walking along together one day. The optimist exclaimed, with a lilt in his voice, "This is simply the best of all possible worlds!"

The pessimist sighed gloomily, "Yeah, you're probably right."

Scripture: Always be prepared to give an answer to everyone who asks you to give the reason for the hope that you have. (1 Peter 3:15 NIV)

Sendoff: To share your hope is to lift life to a higher plane. Find a way to share your deepest hope with someone today.

61. Put on Hold

a mother and daughter walked out of church one Sunday morning. The mother said, "That was a nice service. I really liked the soft piano music during the prayer."

The little girl turned and exclaimed, "Was that a piano?" Her mother nodded affirmatively. Whereupon the child added, "Oh—I thought God had put us on hold."

> *Scripture: The LORD is my shepherd, I shall not want. (Psalm 23:1)*
>
> *Sendoff: God will never withhold goodness and mercy from humanity. Nor will God withhold these things from your life!*

62. Better Than Shopping

*I*t was just a few days before Christmas. Two men who were next-door neighbors decided to go sailing while their wives went Christmas shopping. While the men were out in their sailboat, a storm arose. The sea became very rough, and the men had great difficulty keeping the boat under control.

As they maneuvered their way toward land, they hit a sandbar, and the boat grounded. Both men jumped overboard and began to push and shove with all their strength, trying to get the boat into deeper water. With his legs almost knee-deep in mud, the waves bouncing him against the side of the boat, and his hair blowing wildly in the wind, one of the men said to the other, with a knowing grin, "It sure beats Christmas shopping, doesn't it?"

Scripture: But when the fullness of time had come, God sent his Son, born of a woman, born under the law, in order to redeem those who were under the law, so that we might receive adoption as children. (Galatians 4:4-5)

Sendoff: The most important thing about Christmas is the coming of Jesus into your world and mine.

63. He Made It!

*T*he pastor in a small-town parish was dependent upon parishioners for upkeep and maintenance of the church. He once asked a young father and husband to rewire the confessionals. The only way to reach the wiring was to enter the attic above the altar and crawl over the ceiling by balancing on the rafters. Concerned for her husband's safety, the man's wife waited in the pews.

Unbeknown to both of them, some parishioners were congregating in the vestibule. They paid little attention to the young wife, probably assuming she was praying. Worried about her husband, the wife looked up toward the ceiling and called, "Sam? Sam? Are you up there? Did you make it okay?"

There was quite an outburst from the vestibule when Sam's hearty voice echoed down, "Yes, I made it up here just fine!"

Scripture: Now when all the people were baptized, and when Jesus also had been baptized and was praying, the heaven was opened, and the Holy Spirit descended upon him in bodily form like a dove. And a voice came from heaven, "You are my Son, the Beloved; with you I am well pleased." (Luke 3:21-22)

Sendoff: God, grant me the confirming voice of your will for me. Help me to know you are present and active.

64. The Professor

$\mathcal{T}$he proverbial absent-minded professor encountered a colleague on the campus quad. "Tell me," he said to his peer after they had chatted for a while, "which way was I headed when we met?"

The colleague replied, "I believe you were walking toward your office."

"Good," said the professor, "that means I've had my lunch."

Scripture: Remember the long way that the LORD your God has led you... (Deuteronomy 8:2)

Sendoff: We are constantly enjoined by the Old Testament writers to "remember, and not forget." Memory is a valued part of the faith experience.

65. Good Times

a little boy was heard praying, "Lord, if you can't make me a better boy, don't worry about it; I'm having a real good time like I am."

Scripture: He called a child, whom he put among them, and said, "Truly I tell you, unless you change and become like children, you will never enter the kingdom of heaven." (Matthew 18:2-3)

Sendoff: May I never be fully satisfied with the way I am. May I always desire growth and change in my journey.

66. Male and Female

A schoolteacher, wanting her students to have some contact with the animal world, brought a rabbit to her classroom. The children were delighted, of course, and asked all kinds of questions about rabbits. In the lively exchange, one student inquired whether it was a "boy or girl" rabbit.

The teacher was a bit taken aback at the question and confessed that she did not know. One little girl's face suddenly lit up when she exclaimed, "We could *vote* on it!"

Scripture: Of clean animals, and of animals that are not clean, and of birds, and of everything that creeps on the ground, two and two, male and female, went into the ark with Noah, as God had commanded Noah. (Genesis 7:8-9)

Sendoff: Dear God, thank you for the beauty and power of sexuality in creation.

67. Breakfast Cereal

A seven-year-old daughter was the joy of her father's life. She also kept him on track much of the time. One day the father had worked quite late, but he also had to rise early in the morning to keep an important appointment. As he set the alarm clock, he said to the whole family, "I'm so tired, I probably won't hear this thing go off. So if anybody hears it, be sure to get me up."

Sure enough, he slept through the ringing alarm. So did everyone else except the daughter. She went to wake her father, then went downstairs to fix him some breakfast. She got a bowl, poured in some cold cereal, put sugar and milk on it, and then went back upstairs to wake her father again.

He still responded sleepily, so she went back downstairs. Moments later, she came tearing up the stairs, shook her father, and pleaded, "Get up, Daddy! It's later than it's ever been: Your cereal's sinking!"

> *Scripture: And let people learn to devote themselves to good works in order to meet urgent needs, so that they may not be unproductive. (Titus 3:14)*
>
> *Sendoff: May I be mindful of that which is truly urgent, and may I trust God to help me discern the productive from the unproductive in my life.*

68. He Who Has Ears to Hear...

$\mathcal{A}$ man was perplexed by his wife's refusal to admit her hearing problem. Speaking with his doctor one day, he exclaimed, "How can I get my wife to admit that she is hard of hearing?"

"I'll tell you what you need to do," his doctor replied. "When you arrive home this evening, peek your head through the door and say, 'Hi, honey. What's for dinner tonight?' If she doesn't answer, go into the living room and say again, 'Honey, what's for dinner?' If she still doesn't hear you, walk right up behind her and speak directly in her ear: 'Honey, what's for dinner?' Then you will be able to convince her of her need for a hearing exam."

"Great!" the man responded. "I think it will work."

That evening, the man arrived home from work. Just as he had been instructed, he opened the front door and called out, "Honey, what's for dinner tonight?" He listened carefully, but there was no reply. He walked to the living room and repeated, "Honey, what's for dinner?" He still received no answer. He then walked into the kitchen and asked, "Honey, what's for dinner?" Still, no answer! The man walked right up behind his wife and spoke directly into her ear, "Honey, what's for dinner?"

At this point, his wife turned around and resolutely replied, "For the *fourth time*, I *said* we're having *spaghetti!*"

Scripture: "But my people did not listen to my voice; / Israel would not submit to me. So I gave them over to their stubborn hearts, / to follow their own counsels. O that my people would listen to me, / that Israel would walk in my ways!" (Psalm 81:11-13)

Sendoff: Listening for God is a spiritual art form and a human necessity.

69. Mouse Walk

*T*wo mice decided to stretch their legs and take a stroll one afternoon. They were busy chatting about different varieties of cheese when they rounded a corner and found themselves face-to-face with a large cat. The cat had a gleam in his eye that said, "Ahhh—lunch!"

The cat was just about to pounce on his prey when one of the mice looked the cat in the eye and barked like a dog. The cat was so surprised and frightened that he turned and ran away.

The mouse that barked turned to the other mouse and calmly said, "In times like these, it's nice to know a second language."

Scripture: "So make up your minds not to prepare your defense in advance; for I will give you words and a wisdom that none of your opponents will be able to withstand or contradict." (Luke 21:14-15)

Sendoff: When challenged, God promises to give us appropriate words to speak. These times need a new word from the community of believers.

70. Telling "Them"

a certain woman in one preacher's congregation would regularly meet him at the door after the service and say, "You really *told* them today, Preacher." Never once did she acknowledge that the sermon had reached her personally.

One particularly snowy Sunday, the preacher arrived at church to find only one person in the congregation. It was this woman. He decided to go ahead with the service. He preached a sermon directed specifically at her, using texts such as "judge not, that you be not judged," and such.

He could hardly wait for her comments after the sermon. When the service ended, he greeted her at the door, only to hear her say, "If they had been here today, Preacher, you would have really *told* them."

Scripture: "Do not judge, and you will not be judged. Do not condemn, and you will not be condemned. Forgive, and you will be forgiven." (Luke 6:37 NIV)

Sendoff: Look at someone today through the fresh eyes of one who knows how to forgive. Pray the Scripture text for your own life, and watch your own spiritual health grow.

71. A Tailor's Wisdom

$\mathcal{A}$ man was bothered by a continual ringing in his ears, a flushed face, and bulging eyes. Over a period of three years, he counseled with one doctor after another. No one seemed to know what was wrong or what needed to be done.

One doctor pulled out the man's tonsils, thinking that was the problem. Another doctor removed his appendix, thinking that would do the trick. Yet another pulled his teeth—again, to no avail. He even went to a doctor in Switzerland who administered an exotic goat-gland treatment. Finally, he went to a doctor who said the man had only three months to live, that his was an extremely rare and untreatable disease, and that it was fatal. So the man decided to quit his job, sell all of his belongings, and simply "live it up" for the time that remained.

He went to his tailor to order some new suits and shirts. "After all," he thought, "if I'm going to live it up, I'm going to do it in style." So the tailor took his tape and began obtaining the measurements he needed. When he measured the man's neck, he wrote down "16½."

But the man corrected him. "That's not right. I wear a 15½, not 16½."

So the tailor measured again. Again the measurement showed 16½.

The man was quite upset. "I'm telling you, that's not right. I wear a 15½, I've *always* worn a 15½, and that's the size shirt collar I want. Do you under-stand?"

The tailor said, "Okay, if that's what you want, that's what you will get. But let me tell you something: Just don't come back in a few days complaining that you have ringing ears, a flushed face, and bulging eyes."

Scripture: [The people said to Moses], "Go near, you yourself, and hear all that the LORD our God will say. Then tell us everything that the LORD our God tells you, and we will listen and do it." (Deuteronomy 5:27)

Sendoff: Is God trying to get through to you on some matter of relative urgency right now?

72. Yearning for Company

A woman called her friend to ask how she was feeling. "Terrible," the other woman replied. "My head's splitting, the house is a mess, and I can't wait for the kids to be in school. And it's too hot."

"Listen," said the caller, "go and lie down. I'll come right over to straighten the house and watch the children until your headache goes away. By the way, how is Sam?"

"Sam?" the hurting housewife asked. "Who in the world is *Sam?*"

"Your husband," came the answer.

"But my husband is Bart, not Sam."

The woman who called gasped and stated, "I'm sorry, I must have dialed the wrong number."

After a long pause, with a note of sadness and despair, the desperate other woman asked, "Does that mean you're not coming over?"

Scripture: My eyes are ever toward the LORD, / for he will pluck my feet out of the net. Turn to me and be gracious to me, / for I am lonely and afflicted. / Relieve the troubles of my heart, / and bring me out of my distress. (Psalm 25:15-17)

Sendoff: Sometimes a few moments of silence in prayer can bring both healing and a certain companionship.

73. Mr. Big

*O*ne of those high-powered, take-charge corporation executives was checking into the hospital. Barking orders left and right, he had his own way until he reached the desk of a small, mild-mannered woman at the final check-in process. She typed the man's name on a slip of paper and stuck the paper into the wrist bracelet before he could react.

"What's *this* for?" demanded Mr. Big.

"That," replied the woman, "is so we won't give you to the wrong mommy when you're ready to leave the hospital."

Scripture: For by the grace given to me I say to everyone among you not to think of yourself more highly than you ought to think, but to think with sober judgment, each according to the measure of faith that God has assigned. (Romans 12:3)

Sendoff: Humility is often a difficult but valued virtue.

74. A Backseat Question

a four-year-old boy was in the backseat of the family car, eating an apple. At one point, he asked his father, "Why is my apple turning brown?"

His father proceeded to answer: "It's because after you ate the outer skin of the apple, the 'meat' of the apple came in contact with the air. That, in turn, caused the apple to oxidize. That, in turn, caused a significant color variation that is much darker than it was before."

The child was silent for a moment, and then he looked at his father and said, "Daddy, are you talking to *me?*"

Scripture: "When in the future your child asks you, 'What does this mean?' you shall answer, 'By strength of hand the Lord brought us out of Egypt, from the house of slavery.'" (Exodus 13:14)

Sendoff: Give your child or grandchild answers that lift up the strength of the faith tradition.

75. Strange Race

a tourist riding a moped pulled up alongside a Porsche at a traffic signal. The Porsche driver rolled down his window and asked the moped driver if he wanted to race away from the light. The moped driver laughed and said he had only a few horsepower. But the Porsche driver eventually prevailed.

The light changed, and the Porsche took off with a tremendous roar and blaze of speed. The driver saw the moped rider as a dim speck in the rearview mirror. Suddenly, he realized that the speck was getting larger. Then, in his own blaze of speed, the moped driver raced past the Porsche and became a dim speck down the road ahead.

Then the moped driver started back again and raced the other way past the Porsche. This happened several times. Finally, the two came to a stop beside each other. The Porsche driver rolled down his window a second time. "Friend, what kind of an engine do you have in that thing?"

The other responded, "I'm actually not sure. But I would like to disconnect my suspenders from your outside mirror."

Scripture: Therefore, since we are surrounded by so great a cloud of witnesses, let us also lay aside every weight and the sin that clings so closely, and let us run with perseverance the race that is set before us, looking to Jesus the pioneer and perfecter of our faith. (Hebrews 12:1-2)

Sendoff: This text is the great good news for those who believe. Jesus is all in all.

76. Conscience

a man sent $150 in cash to the Internal Revenue Service, along with an unsigned note that read: "Last year I misrepresented my income, and I have not been able to sleep. Enclosed is $150. If I *still* can't sleep, I'll send the rest."

> *Scripture: But as for [the seeds] in the good soil, these are the ones who, when they hear the word, hold it fast in an honest and good heart, and bear fruit with patient endurance. (Luke 8:15)*
>
> *Sendoff: Honesty in all things is a spiritually healthy policy.*

77. Signs

*H*ere are some captions from actual signs:

- In a computer store window: Out for a quick byte.
- In a restaurant window: Don't stand there and be hungry; come in and get fed up.
- At a bowling alley: Please be quiet; we need to hear a pin drop.
- In a music library: Bach in a minuet.
- In a funeral home: Drive carefully; we'll wait.
- In a maternity clothes shop: We're open on Labor Day.
- In an optometrist's office: If you don't see what you're looking for, you've come to the right place!
- On a scientist's door: Gone fission.
- On a fence: Salesmen welcome; dog food is expensive.
- At a muffler shop: No appointment necessary; we'll hear you coming.
- In a butcher shop: Pleased to meat you.
- In a veterinarian's waiting room: Be back in 5 minutes. Sit! Stay!
- On a music teacher's door: Out Chopin.
- On a garbage truck: We've got what it takes to take what you've got.

Scripture: And [Jesus] sighed deeply in his spirit and said, "Why does this generation ask for a sign? Truly I tell you, no sign will be given to this generation." (Mark 8:12)

Sendoff: Jesus is "the Sign"—the Sign that counts above all.

78. Where Is God?

*T*wo brothers, ages ten and twelve, were constantly getting into trouble. Finally, they were asked to appear in the minister's office, one at a time. The ten-year-old went in and was confronted with increasing intensity by the minister: "Where is God?"

The boy was so terrified that he ran home to his brother, grabbed him, and they went into a closet together where they typically contrived their schemes. The younger brother said quietly to his older brother, "We are in big trouble; somebody has stolen God, and they think *we* did it!"

Scripture: "The LORD himself goes before you and will be with you; he will never leave you nor forsake you. Do not be afraid; do not be discouraged." (Deuteronomy 31:8 NIV)

Sendoff: God is the one steadfast assurance of your life.

79. Loafers

*T*he Sunday-school teacher asked an especially bright student what his favorite Bible story was. The lad replied: "The one where everyone loafs and fishes."

Scripture: [Jesus asked,] "When I broke the five loaves for the five thousand, how many baskets full of broken pieces did you collect?" They said to him, "Twelve." "And the seven for the four thousand, how many baskets full of broken pieces did you collect?" And they said to him, "Seven." Then he said to them, "Do you not yet understand?" (Mark 8:19-21)

Sendoff: God is an abundant provider—always an abundance of enough.

80. Dependability

*L*ife is like a chicken trying to lay an egg on an escalator: As soon as she settles in, the bottom drops out.

> *Scripture: I will lie down and sleep in peace, / for you alone, O LORD, / make me dwell in safety. (Psalm 4:8 NIV)*
>
> *Sendoff: I thank you, God, that I can depend fully upon you at all times.*